Myths AND *Tradeoffs*

The Role of Tests in
Undergraduate Admissions

Steering Committee for the
Workshop on Higher Education Admissions

Alexandra Beatty, M.R.C. Greenwood, and
Robert L. Linn, *editors*

Board on Testing and Assessment
Commission on Behavioral and Social Sciences and Education

and

Office of Scientific and Engineering Personnel

National Research Council

NATIONAL ACADEMY PRESS
Washington, D.C.

National Academy Press • 2101 Constitution Avenue, N.W. • Washington, D.C. 20418

NOTICE: The project that is the subject of this report was approved by the Governing Board of the National Research Council, whose members are drawn from the councils of the National Academy of Sciences, the National Academy of Engineering, and the Institute of Medicine. The members of the committee responsible for the report were chosen for their special competences and with regard for appropriate balance.

The National Academy of Sciences is a private, nonprofit, self-perpetuating society of distinguished scholars engaged in scientific and engineering research, dedicated to the further-ance of science and technology and to their use for the general welfare. Upon the authority of the charter granted to it by the Congress in 1863, the Academy has a mandate that requires it to advise the federal government on scientific and technical matters. Dr. Bruce M. Alberts is president of the National Academy of Sciences.

The National Academy of Engineering was established in 1964, under the charter of the National Academy of Sciences, as a parallel organization of outstanding engineers. It is autono-mous in its administration and in the selection of its members, sharing with the National Acad-emy of Sciences the responsibility for advising the federal government. The National Academy of Engineering also sponsors engineering programs aimed at meeting national needs, encourages education and research, and recognizes the superior achievements of engineers. Dr. William A. Wulf is president of the National Academy of Engineering.

The Institute of Medicine was established in 1970 by the National Academy of Sciences to secure the services of eminent members of appropriate professions in the examination of policy matters pertaining to the health of the public. The Institute acts under the responsibility given to the National Academy of Sciences by its congressional charter to be an adviser to the federal government and, upon its own initiative, to identify issues of medical care, research, and educa-tion. Dr. Kenneth I. Shine is president of the Institute of Medicine.

The National Research Council was organized by the National Academy of Sciences in 1916 to associate the broad community of science and technology with the Academy's purposes of furthering knowledge and advising the federal government. Functioning in accordance with general policies determined by the Academy, the Council has become the principal operating agency of both the National Academy of Sciences and the National Academy of Engineering in providing services to the government, the public, and the scientific and engineering communi-ties. The Council is administered jointly by both Academies and the Institute of Medicine. Dr. Bruce M. Alberts and Dr. William A. Wulf are chairman and vice chairman, respectively, of the National Research Council.

International Standard Book Number 0-309-06597-6

Additional copies of this report are available from:
National Academy Press
2101 Constitution Avenue N.W.
Washington, D.C. 20418
Call 800-624-6242 or 202-334-3313 (in the Washington Metropolitan Area).

This report is also available on line at http://www.nap.edu

Printed in the United States of America

iii

Preface

More than 8 million students enrolled in 4-year, degree-granting postsecondary institutions in the United States in 1996. The multifaceted system through which these students applied to and were selected by the approximately 2,240 institutions in which they enrolled is complex, to say the least; for students, parents, and advisers, it is often stressful and sometimes bewildering. This process raises important questions about the social goals that underlie the sorting of students, and it has been the subject of considerable controversy.

The role of standardized tests in this sorting process has been one of the principal flashpoints in discussions of its fairness. Tests have been cited as the chief evidence of unfairness in lawsuits over admissions decisions, criticized as biased against minorities and women, and blamed for the fierce competitiveness of the process. Yet tests have also been praised for their value in providing a common yardstick for comparing students from diverse schools with different grading standards.

Two units of the National Research Council (NRC), the Office of Scientific and Engineering Personnel (OSEP) and the Board on Testing and Assessment (BOTA) of the Commission on Behavioral and Social Sciences and Education, have been following this discussion and have been concerned about several aspects of it. We have worried not only about the sense of conflict and crisis that pervades the discussion, but also about the many misconceptions regarding standardized test scores that seem to have fueled some of the conflict. OSEP's mission includes assessment of the human resources needed to support science and engineering in the United States, and the office's interests in recruitment, graduate education, and employment have led it to consider broader questions about higher education. BOTA's mission is to provide scientific expertise regarding issues of testing and assessment in education and the workplace, and the board has had particular interest in the uses of tests as policy tools and the civil rights implications of tests. The somewhat different missions of these two NRC units come together in a joint concern about the role of tests in higher education admissions.

BOTA and OSEP agreed to collaborate on an exploratory investigation of the issues involved in tests in the admissions process for higher education. This work builds not only on the interests and concerns of BOTA and OSEP, but also on a history of studies on testing by the National Research Council. Most recently, BOTA's Committee on Appropriate Test Use offered a broad review of the uses—and misuses—of tests in schools. The steering committee's investigation was strongly supported and encouraged by the NRC leadership, in recognition of the unique place of tests in many aspects of students' education and of the intense public debate about testing.

To carry out this work, BOTA and OSEP formed a small steering committee, drawn from the membership of the two units and cochaired by the units' chairs. We organized a workshop to review basic technical information about the two standardized tests that are most widely used in the undergraduate admissions process (the SAT and the ACT) and to explore a variety of perspectives on questions about their use. This workshop, which took place on December 17-18, 1998, brought together researchers who had focused on particular questions about the tests, admissions officers and other administrators from a variety of institutions who discussed pressures on the college admissions system, and thoughtful observers who reflected on key questions from a variety of perspectives.

This report is based on the information presented and discussed at the workshop and the steering committee's deliberations. It has three purposes: to identify and correct some persistent myths about standardized admissions tests and highlight some of the specific tradeoffs that decisions about the uses of tests entail; to present the steering committee's conclusions and recommendations about the role of tests in college admissions; and to lay out several issues about which information would clearly help decision makers, but about which the existing data are either insufficient or need synthesis and interpretation. We believe it will benefit a broad audience of college and university officials, state and other officials and lawmakers, and others who are wrestling with decisions about admissions policies, definitions of merit, legal actions, and other issues.

The workshop and deliberations summarized in this report were held during a time of particularly rapid change in the landscape of collegiate admissions policy, public opinion about fairness and merit in American society, and legal actions regarding racially conscious admissions practices. The steering committee recognized, therefore, that a necessarily brief investigation could not allow us to address all of the issues surrounding the history and current status of test use in higher education. For example, our limited time and resources prevented a detailed and exhaustive examination of test use practices in the vast and complex array of American institutions of higher learning; nor was there time or resources to explore rigorously the strengths and weaknesses of various alternatives to tests, a number of which are at early stages of development and experimentation.

Thus, the steering committee has no illusions that a single report such as this one will settle definitively a debate of such intensity and duration. But we do hope—and believe—that a reminder, in lay terms, of the purposes, capacities, and limitations of the tests will help to clarify the terms of a discussion that has frequently been very acrimonious. We also hope to wave a bright yellow flag of caution in front of those who are making weighty decisions on sometimes shaky technical grounds.

The steering committee is particularly grateful to the six scholars who wrote papers for the workshop. Hunter Breland, Richard Jaeger, Sylvia Johnson, Samuel Lucas, Linda Wightman, and Warren Willingham worked on a tight deadline to provide targeted examinations of key issues we wanted to explore. Their papers were very valuable during the deliberations that resulted in this report. The success of the workshop also depended on the efforts of a number of other scholars and college and university officials. Their thoughtful presentations reflected a variety of important perspectives. Many admissions officers took the time to assist us during a very busy time of the year, and their insights were invaluable. The steering committee extends its heartfelt thanks to them and to the other discussants, presenters, and panelists, who helped to lay out a wide range of issues and contributed to a lively and substantive discussion. Several members of BOTA who did not serve on the steering committee offered advice and assistance at several points and contributed most helpfully at the workshop; we extend our thanks to Richard Atkinson, William Taylor, William Trent, and Lauress Wise.

The steering committee also thanks Michael Feuer and Charlotte Kuh, the directors of BOTA and OSEP, respectively, who provided leadership in the conception and execution of this project, and Alix Beatty, who guided the project throughout and drafted this report. Dorothy Majewski's able administrative assistance with both the workshop and the report are gratefully acknowledged as well.

This report has been reviewed in draft form by individuals chosen for their diverse perspectives and technical expertise, in accordance with procedures approved by the NRC's Report Review Committee. The purpose of this independent review is to provide candid and critical comments that will assist the institution in making the published report as sound as possible and to ensure that the report meets institutional standards for objectivity, evidence, and responsiveness to the study charge. The review comments and draft manuscript remain confidential to protect the integrity of the deliberative process.

We thank the following individuals for their participation in the review of this report: John A. Blackburn, Admissions Office, University of Virginia; Lloyd Bond, Department of Educational Research and Methodology, University of North Carolina, Greensboro; David W. Breneman, School of Education, University of Virginia; Daryl Chubin, Office of Research, Evaluation, and Communication, National Science Foundation; Jonathan R. Cole, Provost and Dean of Faculties, Columbia University; Gene Maeroff, Teachers College, Columbia University; Willie Pearson, Department of Sociology, Wake Forest University; David Pilbeam, Peabody Museum, Harvard University; Henry W. Riecken, Professor of Behavioral Sciences, University of Pennsylvania School of Medicine (emeritus); and Rebecca Zwick, Department of Education, University of California, Santa Barbara.

Although the individuals listed above have provided constructive comments and suggestions, it must be emphasized that responsibility for the final content of this report rests entirely with the authoring committee and the institution.

> M.R.C. Greenwood, *Chair,* Office of Science and
> Engineering Personnel
> Robert L. Linn, *Chair,* Board on Testing and Assessment

Contents

Myths AND Tradeoffs

Executive Summary

College admissions in the United States is both complex and extremely important. The nation prides itself on the provision of public education for all students, and that commitment has been one of the keys to its success as a democracy. College is increasingly seen as a necessary ingredient in the preparation of students for success in a society that requires of its workers both sophisticated skills and the flexibility to adapt quickly to change. Degrees from elite institutions remain the best means of entry into elite, powerful, profitable, and interesting careers. Under these circumstances, it is more important than ever that the college admissions system be both fair and open. Test scores play a role at a number of points in this system: in some cases that role is an intentional and useful one; in others it is an unintended and potentially counterproductive one. Nevertheless, the benefits of tests are clear and lead to our basic conclusions:

- The U.S. educational system is characterized by variety. Public, private, and parochial schools each apply their own standards, and public schools are controlled locally, not nationally. Curricula, grading standards, and course content vary enormously. In such a system, standardized tests are an efficient source of comparative information for which there is currently no substitute.
- Standardized tests can be provided at a relatively low cost to students and offer valuable efficiencies to institutions that must review thousands of applications.
- Standardized tests provide students with an opportunity to demonstrate talent. For students whose academic records are not particularly strong, a high score can lead admissions officers to consider acceptance for a student who would otherwise be rejected.

Yet tests are not always used as they should be. We offer four recommendations to institutions of higher education and one to test producers:

- Admissions policies and practices should be derived from and clearly linked to an institution's overarching intellectual and other goals.
- The use of test scores in the admissions process should serve those institutional goals.

- The admissions policies themselves, and their relationship to the institution's goals, should be clearly articulated for the public, so that students can make informed decisions about whether to apply.

- Colleges and universities should review their uses of test scores in the admissions process and, if necessary, take steps to eliminate misuses of scores. Specifically, institutions should avoid treating scores as more precise and accurate measures than they are and should not rely on them for fine distinctions among applicants.

- Test producers should intensify their efforts to make clear—both in score reports and in documents intended for students, parents, counselors, admissions officers, and the public—the limits to the information that scores supply. This could be done by supplementing the interpretive material currently supplied with clear descriptions and representations—accessible to a lay audience—of such points as the significance of the standard error and the fact that the score is a point on a range of possible scores; the accuracy with which a score can predict future academic performance (in terms of the probability that a student would achieve a particular grade point average, for example); and the significance of score differences.

While these recommendations are modest, it is the committee's hope that they will be of use as the education and legal communities struggle to address the vexing issues surrounding college admissions in the United States.

Context

History

The use of standardized tests in the college admissions process has grown steadily since they were developed early in the twentieth century.[1] These tests grew out of a larger movement to use newly devised measures of mental ability to help address a variety of emerging social problems: the early development of standardized ability testing was characterized in a 1982 National Research Council report as both "a search for order in a nation undergoing rapid industrialization and urbanization, and a search for ability in the sprawling, heterogeneous society that emerged from these processes" (National Research Council, 1982:81). Standardized tests were first used for selection for the civil service and other employment, but their potential value in education was quickly apparent. As student populations grew in the early years of the century, both secondary school and college officials sought means of introducing order in a haphazard system. Colleges were developing increasingly diverse requirements, and secondary schools were providing increasingly diverse preparation. To address this situation, the College Board, formed in 1900, developed a set of essay examinations to assess the preparation, in various subjects, of secondary students from schools around the country.[2]

Continuing population growth and demand for college access soon placed further pressures on the system. The view of college as a privilege for the relative few was giving way to a conception that society needed more educated workers and that a college degree benefited individuals in increasingly practical ways. After World War I, many colleges for the first time received applications from more students than they could accommodate and were forced to select among them. The colleges saw a need for a means of identifying students who were capable of college work, not only those who had completed familiar college preparatory programs

---

[1]Standardized tests are those that are designed to provide all test takers with a uniform experience and an equal opportunity to demonstrate the skills or knowledge being measured. Many kinds of tests, not only multiple-choice ones, can be administered and scored in a standard fashion.

[2]The historical information in this section is drawn from National Research Council (1982:81-96), Wightman and Jaeger (1988:8-12), and U.S. Congress, Office of Technology and Assessment (1992:121-129).

(National Research Council, 1982:92). Advances in ability testing promised to make that identification possible, and the College Board sponsored the development of the first multiple-choice-format Scholastic Aptitude Test (SAT), which was administered in 1926.[3] By the start of World War II, the SAT was a well-established part of the admissions process, and as the century ends it is taken by millions of students every year. Its success inspired the development of similar tests for admission to graduate and professional schools, and by the late 1950s, a competing undergraduate admissions test, the American College Test (ACT).

On average, a college degree offers significant economic and social benefits, and the proportion of high school graduates seeking these benefits has been growing steadily during the twentieth century (National Center for Education Statistics, 1998a:1-2). There are many kinds of institutions with many different missions, and students with a range of strengths and purposes seek college educations. College degrees are not all equally easy to obtain, nor do they offer equal benefits. Demand for places at some institutions, particularly the most prestigious ones, exceeds supply. However, 93 percent of qualified applicants to 4-year institutions are accepted by at least one, and 84 percent enroll (National Center for Education Statistics, 1998b:6).[4] The problems lie primarily not with the possibility of going to any college, but with gaining admission to the competitive ones. At best, the sorting process matches students with colleges in ways that will benefit both; at worst, it perpetuates deep inequalities in American society. The question of fairness has consequently been a perennial part of the discussion of college admissions in the United States.

The Tests

Today, approximately 90 percent of 4-year public and private institutions require applicants to submit admissions test scores (Breland, 1998:7-9).[5] Although institutions make use of a wide variety of other informa-

---

[3]The test is now formally known by its initials alone.

[4]In this context "qualified" applicants are those who have met basic criteria defined by colleges, such as high school graduation and completion of required coursework. Many institutions accept all qualified applicants.

[5]Breland reports that the public and private surveyed institutions ranked high school performance (grade point average or class rank) as the most important factor in admissions, with test scores and exposure to college-level work second and third, respectively.

tion, it is their uses of test scores in particular that have given rise to considerable controversy and confusion. The two tests that supply these scores, the SAT and the ACT, have significant similarities and are viewed by some as almost interchangeable, but they were designed with somewhat different purposes and retain important differences in content and structure. The SAT, originally developed to assist competitive institutions (mostly located on the two coasts), was designed to measure general verbal and mathematical reasoning in order to provide "a standard way of measuring a student's ability to do college-level work" (quoted in Wightman and Jaeger, 1998:5-6). The ACT, in contrast, was designed to assist institutions (mostly in the middle states) that generally admitted all qualified applicants—typically, students who have completed particular course requirements (perhaps achieving a minimum grade point average) and received a high school diploma. Consequently, this newer test was designed to draw more explicitly on the content knowledge students had acquired in high school and to assess how well they could use and apply it. The ACT was intended not only to assist colleges in admissions and recruitment, but also with course placement and academic planning. It had the additional purpose of helping students to "identify and develop realistic plans for accomplishing their educational and career goals" (quoted in Wightman and Jaeger [1998:3] from ACT materials). Thus, a fundamental distinction between the two tests is that the SAT was originally intended to help colleges identify the ablest students for admission to elite institutions, and the ACT was originally intended to provide fairly detailed profiles of the full range of students, to help both students and colleges determine the best academic path for each student.

Although the distinction between the coastal and midwestern institutions that accounted for these differences has faded, the SAT and the ACT have retained their distinct goals (despite the fact that in many institutions the two tests are used almost interchangeably).[6] The SAT is described by its developers as a measurement of reasoning abilities that develop "over years of schooling and in . . . outside reading and study" (quoted in Wightman and Jaeger, 1998:6). It is endorsed by the College Board and the Educational Testing Service as a predictor of academic

---

[6]Some institutions that accept scores from either test use conversion tables to translate scores from one test to the scale of the other, in order to compare the performance of applicants.

success that is useful in admissions decisions, although not as the sole criterion for such decisions. The ACT is also intended as a predictor of success in college, but it is endorsed by its developers for use by high schools in counseling, evaluation studies, accreditation documentation, and public relations; by state and national agencies for financial aid, loan, and scholarship decisions, and other uses; and by colleges for placement and recruitment, as well as admissions decisions.

SAT and ACT scores are currently used in a wide range of ways in a wide range of settings. Some of these uses are technically defensible means of pursuing important goals, but others are not. The steering committee has been guided in its deliberations about these uses by general criteria for appropriate test use that have been defined in the context of previous work by The Board on Testing and Assessment. Of those criteria, the two most relevant to admissions testing are that a test's validity can be understood only in the context of the purpose for which it is being used, and that "no single test score can be considered a definitive measure of a student's knowledge" (National Research Council, 1999:2-3).

Persistent Controversies

The proportion of high school graduates who enroll in college grew from 49 percent in 1979 to 65 percent in 1996 (Breland, 1998:3). Not surprisingly, the proportion of high school graduates who take standardized tests has also risen. These test scores are also frequently put to uses other than those for which they were devised. The tests have indeed become, in the words of Wightman and Jaeger (1998), a "ubiquitous presence" with high stakes attached, so it is not surprising that they have been demonized, lionized, and misunderstood.

There are several reasons that debate and controversy continue to surround the use of admissions tests at selective institutions. A key one is the persistence of score gaps, particularly between white and minority students, but among other groups as well. The black-white score gap on admissions tests, as on most standardized tests, is large, and the proportion of black students in the highest score ranges is low (Kane, 1998:433-435). What do the gaps mean? Are the tests biased against minority students or females or unfair to particular groups in some other way? Do they simply reflect inequities that begin affecting minority students long before they take college admissions tests?

Samuel Lucas reviewed the existing research on explanations for the score gaps, particularly between blacks and whites, for the workshop and made several points that are particularly important in this context. First, although significant score gaps persist, they have shifted: in general, black students' scores have risen significantly in comparison with those of whites since the 1960s, and gaps associated with socioeconomic differences among test takers are sometimes larger than those between black and white students. Lucas also drew a sharp distinction between students' actual ability, which may or may not be revealed through a particular performance, and their demonstration of that ability—through performance on a test, for example—which he called achievement. He noted (Lucas, 1998:3):[7]

> Any given performance, or set of performances, can only reveal, at best, one's level of mastery; it is not possible to reveal one's untapped capacities, which might be far greater than the achievement level demonstrated on the measuring instrument. For this reason, then, by the definition of ability, a test may measure achievement, not ability.

Lucas' point relates to broad questions about uses of test scores and varying interpretations of academic merit. If one views the test score gap as valuable evidence of differing likelihoods of academic success in college for different groups, then relying on the scores as an element in selection makes sense. If, however, one views the gap as a reflection of differences in *prior* accomplishment, then that use may be questioned. For the steering committee, however, this question leapfrogs over the more basic question of whether the test scores in question are sufficiently robust—that is, statistically strong—to bear the weight of the gatekeeping function, regardless of how they are viewed.

Addressing another reason for controversy, Sylvia Johnson discussed at the workshop some of the consequences of the disparities in test scores. Clearly, to the extent that test scores have been used to regulate access to higher education, minority students' lower scores have put them at a disadvantage in the competition for places (Johnson, 1998:13). But the gap may have other, subtler effects, as well. For example, researchers have suggested that students' test performance may be impaired by their aware-

---

[7]Appreciation of this distinction is reflected in the College Board's decision to change the name of its admissions test from the Scholastic Aptitude Test to the Scholastic Assessment Test, and, finally, to the SAT.

ness of negative stereotypes about the group to which they belong (Johnson, 1998:19; see also Steele, 1997; Steele and Aronson, 1995). Thus, Claude Steele and others have argued, knowledge of the performance gap on standardized admissions tests may lower the performance of minority students, contributing to continuance of the gap. Research on uses of other kinds of high-stakes tests also suggests that classification of minority students as low achievers can serve to limit their opportunities to benefit from demanding curricula and other educational opportunities (Johnson, 1998:8-13). Although findings such as these have not been linked to college admissions tests, they do demonstrate the complexity of the discussions of academic merit and the role of tests in defining it.

More practically, the existence of score gaps, particularly between black and white students, is one key reason that affirmative action programs were developed—and are so controversial—since colleges have long sought both academic merit and diverse student populations.[8] Since academic merit has increasingly been defined by test scores, the gap in test performance has made these goals seem starkly opposed. If there were no gap—and if minorities as a group were as well positioned as whites for competitive college selection—the role of test scores in admissions might not have become so controversial. Although being well positioned for college selection involves far more than strong test scores, as selective institutions have long stated in their policies, other performance measures, such as high school records, often show similar gaps. It is important to note that standardized tests are not the sole reason that minorities' access to higher education has been limited. Indeed, affirmative action has been intended as a means of enriching the education of all students by finding means—including the possibility of relaxed requirements for test scores or other criteria—of including diverse, capable individuals from groups that were traditionally underrepresented (or excluded) because of complex historical and cultural inequalities. These inequalities continue to affect educational aspirations and achievement. Moreover, views of the problems raised by test use have to a certain extent been shaped by the context of the United States' long history of racial inequality.

The test score gap fosters the notion that minorities as a group are less qualified for academic success, and it also complicates the use of scores

---

[8]The reasons that colleges seek diversity are discussed below and are also treated in detail in Bowen and Bok (1998).

for selection.[9]   Some institutions have used test scores in formulas and other numerical systems for selecting among applicants; because minority groups score lower than others, on average, colleges have sometimes applied these methods differently for different groups in order to ensure racial diversity in their entering classes.   Some of these uses have been challenged as unfair and illegal; the 1996 legal ruling in Texas's *Hopwood* case and voter actions in both California and Washington have barred public colleges in those jurisdictions from considering race at all as a means of promoting diversity in the admissions process.   It is important, however, to distinguish among the many methods of considering race that have been used. The University of Texas School of Law, for example, (the subject of the *Hopwood* lawsuit) was using an explicit two-track system, under which different selection criteria were used for white and black students.   Many other institutions, however, have simply used race as one among many so-called "plus factors" in the process.

Colleges throughout the nation are reevaluating their admissions policies in light of the outcomes of court cases and voters' mandates and waiting to see what effects the changes will have on the institutions that are subject to them.   Many colleges want to know whether they are vulnerable to legal challenge themselves, and many are also taking the opportunity to reflect more broadly on their reasons for seeking culturally and ethnically diverse student populations, the goals underlying their admissions practices, and the extent to which their practices serve their goals.

In this climate of rapid change and reevaluation, an objective look at what is known about the current admissions process, and about the strengths and limitations that standardized tests bring to it, is important.

---

[9]One reason that the existence of the gap between minority and majority students' scores will inevitably complicate the use of scores in selection is the statistical phenomenon that lower scorers (regardless of who they are) are more likely to fall in the "false negative" category—that is, more likely to not be selected though they actually have the capacity to succeed—than are higher scorers. This phenomenon is not a reflection of cultural bias on tests, but it is a potential source of disparate impact on minorities when they score lower on average. This phenomenon is explained in detail in Messick (1993:78-80); see also American Educational Research Association et al. (1998). Test scores typically overpredict black students' college performance (Vars and Bowen, 1998:465-466).

What Do Colleges Really Do?

U.S. colleges and universities could hardly be less uniform. There are state universities with tens of thousands of students and liberal arts colleges with fewer than a thousand. There are institutions that place particular emphasis on excellence in science and technology, the arts, study of the classics, preparation for particular occupations, or other endeavors. Some admit only women; others have traditionally served African Americans. Some are revered around the world; others are barely known outside their home states. They vary also in their sources of financial support, their resources, their needs, and their problems. Not surprisingly, their admissions procedures reflect these differences, as each institution attempts to identify and admit the group of students that will best enable it to fulfill its mission.

It is important to note at the outset of this discussion that although a variety of information about what admissions officers do is available, there is clearly a limit to what can be known, in a scientific sense, about the process and the range of practices. Ultimately, a variety of individuals are asked to make decisions on the basis of particular sets of circumstances and available information. Statistics and other formal methods of inquiry can only partly explore a process of this kind.

A fundamental question about the admissions policy at any school is how selective it is, but every institution that can admit fewer students than apply will seek a particular balance in the selected pool. Figure 1 illustrates the varying selectivity of U.S. institutions. Factors that may be weighed as institutions deliberate about admissions decisions include the needs of different academic departments; overall goals for academic quality; a desire for athletes, musicians, campus leaders, and the like; a desire to maintain alumni loyalty, by accepting legacy students, for financial and other reasons; a desire for geographical and gender balance; and a desire for racial and ethnic diversity. Every institution strikes its own balance among these and other factors, and the right of institutions to do so has been explicitly upheld by the Supreme Court in its 1978 ruling in the Bakke case. The court found that institutions can define educational criteria, including racial diversity, that they wish to consider in admissions,

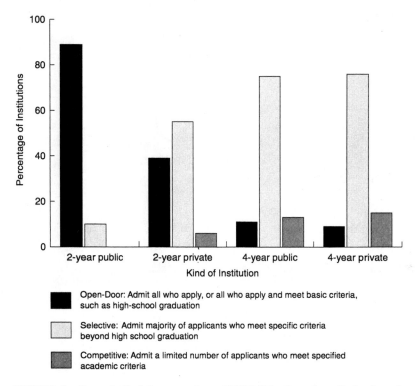

FIGURE 1   General admissions practices. SOURCE: Data from Breland et al. (1995:9-10).

so long as they do not apply different standards to different groups *(Regents of the University of California v. Bakke,* 438 U.S. 265, 1978).[1]

To achieve their institutional goals, admissions officers do a great many things, including, but not limited to: using numerical formulas based on grade point averages (GPAs), test scores, and class rankings; interviewing students; reading student essays and recommendations; consulting with faculty and other administrators; recruiting individual students or categories of students; reviewing the performance of students

---

[1]The Bakke decision applies to public institutions throughout the United States except in areas in which it has been explicitly superceded: the region served by the fifth court circuit, which decided the Hopwood case, and states that have passed referenda limiting affirmative action, California and Washington.

admitted in previous years; and conducting market research. Institutions that accept most of their applicants face far fewer challenges than highly selective institutions do, but when admissions officers speak and write about what they do in composing classes, they frequently make the point that it is more an art than a science. The process that has evolved is quite messy and complex, and it often puzzles and frustrates those who try to understand it. Although it is likely that almost anyone involved in the process would agree that it ought to be "fair," applying that standard to so complex a process is far less simple than its users might wish.

It is the criteria of the most selective schools that are often the most difficult to fathom, precisely because their popularity makes their selection processes so difficult. The most selective institutions are only a small fraction of U.S. colleges, and the great majority of students are admitted to the institution of their choice. It is important to note, however, that a degree from a highly selective school confers significant benefits. The recent investigation of the effects of affirmative action by William Bowen and Derek Bok, *The Shape of the River*, for example, documents "a real wage premium associated with enrollment at an academically selective institution," as well as other, more qualitative benefits, and others have found similar results (Bowen and Bok, 1998:128; see also Kane, 1998:440-448).[2]   Given these benefits, as well as the countless other factors that contribute to institutional reputations, it is no wonder that some institutions attract as many as eight or ten candidates for every available place. Because a majority of the self-selected applicants for these institutions are academically strong, such schools can hardly rely on numerical formulas in composing their freshman classes.

However difficult it may seem for institutions to explain the other criteria they use, many voices are currently arguing that they still bear a responsibility to be candid. A school may prize the highest academic achievement for all its students (and use numerical formulas as the primary indicator of potential for that achievement) and therefore generally admit only students who score above a certain level. However, such an institution is still likely to need to select from a pool that meets that

---

[2]More specifically, Bowen and Bok show (1998:450) that for the 1976 graduating class, attendance at one of the 28 selective institutions they studied yielded significantly higher salaries in comparison with those of B.A. holders nationwide. The wage premium holds for blacks and whites and for men and women.

criterion—that is, it will not be able to accept all the students who meet it. Moreover, most institutions reserve the right to admit students who do not meet that criterion because they want to make room for students with extraordinary artistic talent, or who have overcome a significant adversity, or who can help meet an institutional goal in some other way. A common analogy for what admissions officers, particularly at the most selective schools, must do in constructing a class is to the formation of an orchestra. If the only criterion for selecting the musicians were technical mastery, the orchestra could end up, by chance, with an oversupply of violinists and not a single clarinetist or flutist. Just as an orchestra leader must consider the kinds of music the orchestra plays, the demands of its audiences, and many other factors in selecting musicians, selective colleges must consider more than quantitative measures of academic potential in composing their classes.

Some colleges, of course, confront different admissions problems. Many large state institutions, for example, rely heavily on numerical formulas because it is their policy to accept most or all qualified applicants. The formulas are used to efficiently identify students who meet the qualifications, which generally include such criteria as meeting a minimum GPA in specific courses. Such schools often have complex eligibility requirements for individual departments, required placement tests, and other means of sorting admitted students, and these separate processes have their own implications for fairness. However, the admissions procedures are often quite straightforward, and these institutions rely on formulas not for selection, but to identify among the thousands of applicants they receive those students who meet all of their stated criteria.

Many selective institutions also receive thousands of applications, and admissions officers are quick to point out that the practical issues they face vary a great deal from place to place. For example, a small school such as Hampshire College in Massachusetts has eight admissions officers to review approximately 2,200 applications (for a class of approximately 370) or one officer for every 275 applicants. Because of this low ratio, the admissions officers have time to read all the applications, particularly the essays, carefully; to call the authors of student recommendations with questions; and to do many other things of which many of their counterparts could only dream. (The tuition at Hampshire is also at the high end of the spectrum.) Submitting test scores is optional for Hampshire, and the college's efforts to foster diversity are integrated into its thorough review of the individuals who apply, as well as its recruitment efforts.

An example of another kind of institution is the University of Wisconsin, which has a staff of 13 to process some 17,000 freshman applications (for a class of approximately 5,400) or one officer for every 1,300 applications. The university has sufficient places to automatically admit students with the highest scores and grades without necessarily reviewing their files; it faces few of the troubling choices among apparently equally well-prepared candidates that face more prestigious institutions that attract a high volume of applications from across the country. The university increasingly relies on energetic recruiting and efforts to improve their yield—that is, the rate at which accepted students decide to enroll—as a means of building and maintaining diversity. At the small number of institutions with international reputations, the issues are somewhat different. The popularity and distinguished academic reputations of schools such as Harvard, Yale, and Stanford, for example, mean that students with top test scores and other accomplishments on their records are frequently turned away. For these institutions the problem is one of composing a balanced class from a large pool of outstanding applicants.

It is important to bear in mind, in considering the range of college admission practices, the range of possible goals institutions may be pursuing. For example, academic goals might range from enrolling students who will complete the coursework and graduate to enrolling a high percentage of students who will achieve academic distinction and pursue graduate study. Social goals might include meeting the needs of local employers, fostering a commitment to social service, and populating the professions with minority students. Most institutions have multiple goals. Even top research universities, for example, do not see their purpose as solely to prepare undergraduates for careers in academia, but rather to prepare them for a range of careers, and institutions of all sorts pride themselves on the range of accomplishments achieved by their graduates, as well as on the quality of the undergraduate experience they provide.

Some accounts of approaches to admissions at individual schools are available, but relatively little is known about the range of specific practices and the extent to which they vary. Surveys conducted by the American Association of Collegiate Registrars and Admissions Officers, the College Board, Educational Testing Service, American College Testing, and others have answered some basic questions and provided intriguing aggregate data about test takers, test use, and other practices. A paper prepared by Hunter Breland (1998) for the workshop documents these efforts, including two important findings: the percentage of institutions requiring test scores has hovered around 90 percent at least since the late 1970s, and private institutions weigh factors such as letters, interviews, essays, or personal qualities significantly more heavily than do public institutions. Breland also shows that public institutions report making exceptions to academic requirements for minorities, students with special talents, and athletes, at a significantly higher rate than do private institutions.

Yet fine-grained information about the range of practices and the extent to which they comport with existing professional standards is elusive. Virtually all institutions provide public announcements of their admissions requirements, which often include general statements about institutional goals. What is less common is a public statement that includes a detailed and nuanced picture of the admissions process. In the absence of specific information about the kinds of criteria that most interest a school and the educational goals that dictate those criteria, students and their advisers frequently rely on other sources—most particularly, published rankings that weigh quantitative factors fairly heavily—in deciding where to apply. These published rankings, and other sources of information about colleges, can mislead students about their prospects.

In the current litigious climate, many institutions are fearful that being too candid about their selection process will only lead to public excoriation and lawsuits, but there are several reasons why such candor would be beneficial. First, the initial step in making a candid statement would be an inventory of the procedures to be described and a frank assessment of how fair they are, how legal they are, how effective they are, and how well they serve the intellectual goals of the institution.

A second benefit of such candor would accrue to potential applicants. Students who know that their test scores are significantly below the average score for entering freshmen at an institution will likely be discouraged from applying. But if students also know that although the institution considers test scores, it also has a particular interest in students who have, for example, demonstrated dedication and talent in the arts, significant academic improvement during the high school years, or a commitment to social service, they could assess their prospects more accurately. Institutions, in turn, would have the opportunity to consider more students with the characteristics they desire. If institutions have articulated their missions clearly, having applications from more such students will enhance their ability to pursue their goals.

Finally, a clear articulation of the institutional goals that drive admissions policies can reveal new perspectives on both what is desirable and what is possible. Many of the institutions that have been compelled by law to change their practices with regard to race have been resourceful in finding new ways to achieve diversity. Expenditures that may previously have seemed out of the question—providing the resources for individual review of each application, for example—may look more reasonable in light of a reframing of the goals for the process and the restrictions on it.

Our review of these potential benefits has led the steering committee to make three recommendations to institutions:

- Admissions policies and practices should be derived from and clearly linked to an institution's overarching intellectual and other goals.
- The use of test scores in the admissions process should serve those institutional goals.
- The admissions policies themselves, and their relationship to the institution's goals, should be clearly articulated for the public, so that students can make informed decisions about whether to apply.

What Do Test Scores Really Mean?

Test scores weigh heavily in many admissions decisions. While published college rankings provide average freshman class scores for individual schools, schools use the scores they receive in a wide variety of ways. As we have noted, arguments about many of these uses have landed in courtrooms across the nation and will likely soon be heard by the Supreme Court. The tests that provide these scores, however, are complicated instruments with specific purposes, and their technical characteristics are not as well understood as they should be, given their important role.

Perhaps the most pervasive misconception about both the SAT and the ACT is that they are precisely calibrated scientific measures (akin to scales or thermometers) of something immutable: ability. A score on either test is, in the eyes of many people, a statement of the individual's intellectual capacity as pitiless and mutely accurate as the numbers denoting his or her height or weight. Although most students who take an admissions test more than once know that scores fluctuate, even very small score differences will seem significant if the measure is regarded as very precise. One consequence of the misconception is that it contributes to misunderstandings in volatile discussions of fairness. Test scores are often used as key evidence in support of claims that an admissions decision was unfair: that is, if student X's score was higher than that of student Y, admitting student Y but not student X was unfair. This argument rests on two important assumptions that deserve examination: that the test measures the criterion that should bear the greatest weight in an admissions decision and that the score is a precise measure of this criterion. To evaluate these assumptions, it is necessary to begin with a closer look at the content of the tests and at the available evidence regarding their statistical properties. The first step is to recognize the important differences between the tests—although many of the individual items on the two tests may look quite similar, the scores represent different approaches to the task of predicting academic success.

The SAT

The SAT I was conceived as a means of identifying the likelihood that students with a wide range of academic preparation could successfully do college-level work.[1]   It was designed to measure verbal and mathematical reasoning by means of multiple-choice questions. (The mathematics section also includes some machine-scorable items in which the students generate answers and record them on a grid.)   In its current form, the test devotes 75 minutes to the verbal section and 60 minutes to the mathematics section.[2] The verbal questions are of three kinds (descriptions from College Board materials quoted in Jaeger and Wightman, 1998:32):

- analogy questions, which assess "knowledge of the meaning of words, ability to see a relationship in a pair of words, and ability to recognize a similar or parallel relationship;
- sentence completion questions, which assess "knowledge of the meaning of words" and "ability to understand how the different parts of a sentence fit logically together;" and
- critical reading questions, which assess "ability to read and think carefully about several different reading passages."

The mathematics section also has several question or item types, all of which contribute to the goal of assessing "how well students understand mathematics, how well they can apply what is known to new situations, and how well they can use what they know to solve nonroutine problems" (Wightman and Jaeger, 1998:34). Each of the sections generates a score on a scale of 200 to 800; thus, the combined scores range from 400 to 1600. No subscores are calculated. Because of the procedures used to ensure that scores from different administrations[3] of the test can be com-

---

[1]SAT I and SAT II are the current names for what used to be two separate testing programs, the SAT, Scholastic Aptitude Test, and the Achievement Tests. The SAT II (Achievement Testing Program) is a set of tests in academic subjects. Though these tests are used in the college admissions process, their role varies widely and has not generated the controversies that the SAT I has; they are not addressed in this report.

[2]The test has evolved since it was first introduced, but its current basic format has been in place since the 1950s; it was modestly revised in the early 1990s, when antonym questions were dropped and sentence completion questions were introduced. The test was statistically "recentered" in 1990s; the steering committee did not address the recentering.

[3]Each time the test is "administered," that is, each time students take it, new versions of the test are used. The tests are constructed to present completely equivalent challenges every time.

pared, it is actually possible to score 800 without answering all of the questions correctly.

The fact that neither section is intended to draw on specific knowledge of course content is the foundation for the claim that the test provides an equal opportunity for students from any school to demonstrate their abilities. Reading passages, for example, include contextual information about the material, and all questions are meant to be answerable without "outside knowledge" of the content. Supporters argue that the test thus ameliorates disparities in school quality. Others have criticized it for precisely this reason, arguing that a test that is independent of curriculum sends the message to students that effort and achievement are less significant than "innate" ability.

The ACT

The ACT, first administered in 1959, has a different design. First, there are more parts to it. In addition to multiple-choice tests of "educational development," which are the basis for the score, students also complete two questionnaires that cover the courses they have taken; their grades, activities, and the like; and a standardized interest inventory.

The test battery has four parts:

• a 45-minute, 75-item English test that yields subscores (that is, scores on a portion of the domain covered by a subset of the test questions) in usage/mechanics and rhetorical skills, as well as an overall score;
• a 60-minute, 60-item mathematics test that yields an overall score and three subscores, in pre-algebra and elementary algebra, intermediate algebra and coordinate geometry, and plane geometry and trigonometry;
• a 35-minute, 40-item reading test that yields an overall score and two subscores, for arts and literature and social sciences and science; and
• a 35-minute, 40-item science reasoning test that yields only a total score. It addresses content "likely to be found in a high school general science course" drawn from biology, chemistry, physics, geology, astronomy, and meteorology.

Each of the four tests is scored on a scale from 1 to 36 (subscores within the tests are on a 1 to 18 scale); the four scores are combined into a composite score on the 1 to 36 scale.

Benefits

We turn now to the assumption that the score on an admissions test should be given the greatest weight in the selection process. Performance on both the SAT and ACT is used as an indicator of how well students are likely to do in college. This outcome is most frequently measured by freshman-year grade point average, and numerous studies have been conducted with data from both tests to determine how well their scores do predict freshman grades—that is, their predictive validity. Warren Willingham provided an overview of current understandings of predictive validity for the workshop. In practice, both tests have an average correlation with first-year college grades that ranges from .45 to .55 (a perfect correlation would be 1.0).[4] The correlations vary for a number of reasons, and research suggests that several factors work to make them seem lower than they actually are. Most important of these is selection bias. Student self-selection restricts the pool of applicants to any given institution, and it is only the scores and grades of the students who were selected from that pool that are used to calculate predictive validity. Since those students are very likely to be academically stronger than those not selected, the capacity of tests and scores to have predicted the rejected students' likely lower performance does not enter into the equation. In addition, freshman grades are not based on uniform standards, but on often subjective judgments that vary across disciplines and institutions; this factor also tends to depress the tests' predictive validity (Willingham, 1998:3, 6-8). This point also underscores the problems with using freshman-year grades as the criterion variable; like the test scores themselves, GPAs that are calculated to two decimal points lend this measure a deceptively precise air. They are used as the criteria for prediction because there is no superior alternative.

Most colleges rely in admissions as much (or more) on high school GPAs or class rank as they do on test scores, and the predictive validity of both numbers together is higher than that of either one alone (Willingham, 1998:8). It is important to note that the high school GPAs are also a "soft" measure—grading standards range as widely at that level as they do in college. However, GPAs reflect several years of performance, not just several hours of testing time. Using high school grades and test

---

[4]More specifically, the amount of variance in predicted outcome is given by r-squared, so a correlation of .50 explains 25 percent of the variance in predicted grades.

scores together is very useful specifically because they are the sources of different kinds of information about students, and "two measures are better than one" (Willingham, 1998:16). Moreover, because both SAT and ACT scores generally predict slightly higher college grades for minority students than they actually receive, "it is not clear that the answer to minority group representation in higher education lies in improved prediction. . . . The challenge is not conventional academic prediction but rather to find valid, socially useful, and workable bases for admitting a broader range of talent" (Willingham, 1998:19-20).

Few colleges would define successful students only by the criterion of their freshman year GPA. One study has shown that other, qualitative measures—specifically high school honors, school reference, applicant's essay, and evidence of persistence—have been used to identify students likely to be successful in broader ways more explicitly related to institutional goals (see Willingham, 1998:14). Although institutions may have success with such efforts, it is clear that test scores and GPAs provide reliable and efficient information that many admissions officers could not easily do without. But test scores were not designed to provide information about all of the factors that influence success in college, which is why test developers specifically recommend that a student's score be used as only one among many criteria considered in the admission process.

It is well known that conflicting impulses motivated the pioneers of college admissions tests—some hoped to open the nation's ivory towers to able students from diverse backgrounds while others sought "scientific" means of excluding particular groups (see Lemann [1995a, 1995b], for a detailed account of the thinking of some of the pioneers). The legacy of association with now-discredited theories about racial differences, and with xenophobic and racist policies of the early twentieth century, lends impact to still-common charges that standardized tests are biased against minority groups and women (National Research Council, 1982:87-93). However, whatever the problems in the construction of earlier instruments, a considerable body of research has explored the possibility of bias in the current admissions tests, and it has not substantiated the claim that test bias accounts for score disparities among groups (see Jencks, 1998).

The steering committee concludes that the standardized tests available today offer important benefits that should not be overlooked in any discussion about changing the system:

• The U.S. educational system is characterized by variety. Public, private, and parochial schools each apply their own standards, and public schools are controlled locally, not nationally. Curricula, grading standards, and course content vary enormously. In such a system, standardized tests are an efficient source of comparative information for which there is currently no substitute.

• Standardized tests can be provided at a relatively low cost to students and offer valuable efficiencies to institutions that must review thousands of applications.

• Standardized tests provide students with an opportunity to demonstrate talent. For students whose academic records are not particularly strong, a high score can lead admissions officers to consider acceptance for a student who would otherwise be rejected.

Limitations

Both the SAT and ACT cover relatively broad domains that most observers would likely agree are relevant to the ability to do college work. Neither, however, measures the full range of abilities that are needed to succeed in college; important attributes not measured include, for example, persistence, intellectual curiosity, and writing ability. Moreover, these tests are neither complete nor precise measures of "merit"—even academic merit. Consequently, the assumption that either test measures the criterion that should bear the greatest weight in admissions is flawed. Both tests provide information that can help admissions officers to make sense of other information in a student's record and to make general predictions about that student's prospects for academic success. The task of constructing a freshman class, however, requires additional information.

The second assumption on which many claims of unfairness rest—that the score is a precise measure—is also weak. A particular score summarizes a student's performance on a particular set of items on a particular day. If a student could take a test 50 or 100 times, his or her scores would vary (even if the student neither learned nor forgot anything between test administrations). Thus, assuming that the test is a valid measure of the targeted skills and knowledge, his or her performance (on those skills and that knowledge) could be described by this range. Ranges can overlap, as is illustrated in Figure 2, which shows the hypothetical performance of two students in multiple administrations of comparable forms

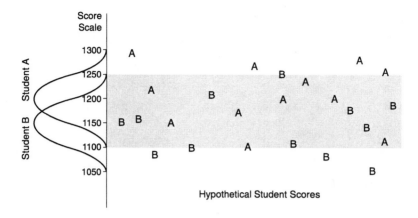

FIGURE 2 Hypothetical score ranges for students A and B. See text for discussion.

of the SAT. Student A, whose scores across many administrations would average 1200, would earn scores ranging between 1100 and 1300, and student B, who averaged 1150, would earn scores ranging between 1050 and 1250. Chance could dictate that any one of student A's many potential scores would be the one he or she actually received and submitted to colleges, as is true for student B (the shaded area indicates the potential overlap). Either student could seem to be the higher scorer.[5] Thus, comparing any two students' scores can be misleading unless they are quite far apart.

Another way of looking at this point is to consider that only fairly large differences in scores could be of use in distinguishing among students who could and could not undertake the work at a particular institution. Using data collected from eleven very selective institutions, Vars and Bowen calculated that "the coefficient on the combined SAT score [verbal plus mathematics] implies that a 100-point increase in SAT score (for example, from 1100 to 1200) raises a student's predicted GPA by roughly 0.11 (from 3.0 to 3.11, for example)" (Vars and Bowen, 1998:463-464). In other words, even a school that has determined that the GPA predicted

---

[5]Assuming a standard error of measurement for the total SAT score of 43 with these hypothetical sets of scores, the probability that student B would score higher than student A on a particular administration of the test is approximately .20: that is, it would happen one time in five.

by test scores is the criterion about which it cares the most would be on shaky ground in using a test score alone to discriminate among students whose scores are even relatively close together. A different sort of test— for example, a licensure exam designed to identify as potential air traffic controllers students who had mastered a specific minimum body of material—could be used to discriminate among students whose scores are quite close together. But such a test would have a cutoff score derived from a clear articulation of the knowledge necessary to perform the job safely and would likely contain many questions targeted toward refining the discrimination around the cutpoint. Such a test would be useful for identifying those who can and cannot perform particular tasks, but not for spreading all the test takers on a scale.[6]

Neither the SAT nor the ACT was designed to make fine distinctions at any point on their scales; rather, both were designed to spread students out across the scales, and both are constructed to provide a balance of questions at a wide range of difficulty levels. These tests are most useful, then, for sorting an applicant pool into broad categories: those who are quite likely to succeed academically at a particular institution, those who are quite unlikely to do so, and those in the middle. Such categories are likely to be defined differently by different institutions, depending on the rigor of their programs and their institutional goals. As Warren Willingham (1998:21) concluded about this point:

> In the early stages of the admissions process, the [predictive] validity of school grades and test scores is put to work through college recruitment, school advising, self-selection, and college selection. In the process, applicants disperse to institutions that differ widely. . . . In later stages of the admissions process, colleges . . . have already profited from the strong validity of these traditional academic predictors. At this point colleges face decisions among applicants in a grey area. . . . This is the time when decisions must ensure that multiple goals of a college receive adequate attention.

Given that a score is a point in a range on a measure of a limited domain, the claim that a higher score should guarantee one student preference over another is not justifiable. Thus, schools that rely too heavily on scores to distinguish among applicants are extremely vulnerable to the charge of unfairness. Any institution is justified in looking beyond scores

---

[6]This kind of test is also subject to error, of course, particularly for scores close to the cutoff score.

and GPAs in the interest of achieving educational goals—and this is as true for the rejection of a high-scoring applicant as for the acceptance of a low-scoring one—assuming it is equally willing to do so for every applicant.

As stated above, the steering committee has concluded that test scores have value in the admissions process. However, test scores are also sometimes used in ways that are not in line with their designs or stated purposes; beyond their technical capacities; or detrimental to important widely shared goals for the process, that is, that it be fair, open, and effective. More specifically, the steering committee has identified two persistent myths that have skewed the debate:

Myth: What admissions tests measure is a compelling distillation of academic merit that should have dominant influence on admissions decisions.

Reality: Admissions tests provide a convenient snapshot of student performance useful only in conjunction with other evidence.

Myth: Admissions tests are precise measures of understanding of the domains they cover.

Reality: Admissions tests are estimates of student performance with substantial margins of error.

In light of the limitations of the available standardized tests, the steering committee makes two recommendations:

• Colleges and universities should review their uses of test scores in the admissions process, and, if necessary, take steps to eliminate misuses of scores. Specifically, institutions should avoid treating scores as more precise and accurate measures than they are and should not rely on them for fine distinctions among applicants.

• Test producers should intensify their efforts to make clear—both in score reports and in documents intended for students, parents, counselors, admissions officers, and the public—the limits to the information that scores supply. This could be done by supplementing the interpretive material currently supplied with clear descriptions and representations—accessible to a lay audience—of such points as the significance of the standard error and the fact that the score is a point on a range of possible scores; the accuracy with which a score can predict future academic performance (in terms of the probability that a student will achieve a particular GPA, for example); and the significance of score differences.

Other Uses of Tests

Test scores have influenced the admissions system in the United States in some indirect but complex ways that also deserve examination. The selectivity of U.S. colleges is not a pure reflection of the respect accorded to their academic output. Rather, it is generally thought of in such terms as the ratio of students accepted to students who apply and of the average test scores of admitted classes. In recent years, rankings of U.S. colleges, particularly the one published by *U. S. News and World Report*, which assigns a relatively heavy weight to test scores, has fostered competition, especially among institutions in the top tier.[7] This circumstance affects the system in several important ways.

For many colleges there are strong incentives to rank high and to maintain or increase the levels of competitiveness they have established—no one wants to seem to be declining in prestige—and public recognition of selectivity can also affect recruitment, alumni support, and other issues about which administrators are quite concerned. Unfortunately, the rankings also provide incentives for schools to encourage a large volume of applications, despite the fact that the large volume increases the difficulty of the selection process.

The strength of the competitive pressure, and how much it varies, can only be guessed at, but admissions officers and other administrators know that it would be possible to manipulate their policies in ways that would affect their rankings if they chose to do so. For example, Tom Parker, the director of admissions at Williams College, explained at the workshop that with the pool of applicants the school currently receives, it would be possible to admit a class that "has average SAT scores 100 points higher than Harvard." However, he noted, they could also alter their procedures in order to affect selectivity (by encouraging applicants who are very unlikely to be accepted) or yield (by discouraging those same applicants

---

[7]A website devoted to the *U. S. News and World Report* rankings provides details about how they are calculated. Test scores are worth 40 percent of a ranking for "student selectivity," which is worth 15 percent of the overall ranking. "Acceptance rate," the ratio of students admitted to number of applicants, is worth an additional 15 percent of the "student selectivity" measure (see http://www.usnews.com/usnews/edu/college/rankings/weight.htm).

and targeting others). Other admissions officers at the workshop concurred that these things are possible. None of those who spoke at the workshop advocated such actions, but virtually all acknowledged the pressures.

It is likely that test scores also play a significant role in the decisions students make about the schools to which they will apply, and it is worth noting that students' self-selection is a significant factor in their access to higher education. Most students see their first scores when they are in the 11th grade or earlier, and they have ample opportunity to compare them to the mean scores at various colleges. A decision not to apply to a particular school may make a great deal of sense if the criteria on which students are evaluated are extremely clear. For a nonselective public institution, the criteria are likely to be straightforward eligibility requirements, and the decision of whether to apply is likely to be straightforward as well. At a more selective institution, however, the criteria are likely to be far more complex and opaque to an aspiring student. The tendency for lower scoring students to opt out of competition at highly selective schools is likely to have a disparate effect on minorities since they have lower average test scores. This tendency is also likely to limit selective schools' opportunity to consider some of the very students they might want to recruit.

Uses of test scores outside of the selection process have effects as well. Scores have been used to identify talented middle-school students for academic enrichment programs and other similar purposes for which they were not intended. Scores calculated for neighborhoods, geographic regions, and the nation as a whole are cited as indicators of academic success and school quality and can even influence real estate values. Comparisons of the average SAT scores of black and white students are also cited as evidence of the advantage given to black applicants at particular institutions (Bowen and Bok, 1998:15-16). However, because black students are underrepresented among high scorers, their average scores would be lower if the selection process were completely race blind. Thus, the fact that black students are in fact underrepresented among high scorers at selective institutions is not evidence of anything in particular about selection at those institutions. Such uses of test scores only further dilute public understanding of standardized admissions tests, distorting the picture of both their benefits and their limitations.

Tradeoffs

The use of test scores to support the claim that an admissions decision is unfair is, in a sense, a distraction from the actual source of contention in such arguments. Test scores have served as an irresistible shorthand for the elusive "merit" that makes a student desirable to colleges. But what colleges desire in the groups of students they enroll each year is, of course, far more complex than one number, or several, could express. Reliance on this shorthand has distorted the discussion in several ways. For one, as we have noted, the seemingly precise character of test scores has made it easy for many people to think of them as conveying rights of access—to believe that a higher scoring student is automatically more deserving of admission than is a lower scoring one. For another, the equating of scores with merit has helped to obscure the complex reasons that colleges have tried by a variety of means—fair and foul—to ensure that they enroll racially and ethnically diverse student populations.

The access of African Americans to higher education in the United States has been extraordinarily limited until very recent times for well-known historical reasons. *The Shape of the River* opens with a statistical portrait of the "predicament" African Americans have faced, noting, for example, that the percentage of that group graduating from college rose from 1.6 percent in 1940 to 5.4 percent in 1960 (Bowen and Bok, 1998:2). The book goes on to describe the growth of race-conscious measures and government efforts to encourage colleges to go beyond simply allowing African Americans to enroll and affirmatively seek to increase minority enrollment. But as this book and many other observers of the situation have been at pains to make clear, colleges seek diverse populations not simply to make amends for past discrimination, but in an effort to achieve specific, important benefits, which include:

- ethnically and racially diverse student populations foster intellectually stimulating exchanges of ideas and perspectives.
- the experience of studying and learning in a diverse environment prepares all students to function in a diverse society.
- employers desire graduates who have learned to cooperate and collaborate with others.
- society benefits in both specific and general ways from a diverse supply of educated graduates who can populate the professions, play a role in civic life, serve as role models, and the like.

These benefits fit closely with other common educational goals, such as developing in students high academic achievement, the capacity to continue learning outside of school, and the ambition to contribute to society. The controversies about tests have grown out of the need to translate such institutional goals into practical and fair means of selecting students. Many people are uncomfortable with the notion of taking race explicitly into account in admissions decisions, and many fear that doing so violates constitutional principles. Unfortunately, as Tom Kane discussed in his presentation at the workshop (based on Kane, 1998), it is very difficult to achieve educational goals that depend on racial and ethnic diversity without taking race explicitly into account in admissions. Ideally, a process that is race blind but yields racial diversity as an outcome would solve the problem. No such process is currently available, so there is a need for compromise between two compelling values.

Because the most selective institutions place heavy emphasis on test scores and high school grades and because minorities are underrepresented among those who do well on both of these measures, Kane argues, race-blind admissions policies at selective institutions would likely yield significantly lower rates of admission for those groups, and this is precisely what has happened at institutions that have been prohibited from considering race.[1] Some have suggested that using demographic factors that frequently correlate with minority status, such as family income or wealth, could be a means of achieving the desired diversity without the need to consider applicants' races. However, although African Americans and Hispanics are more likely than other groups to come from low-income families, they are still a minority of the low-income population, and they are an even smaller minority of the population of the highest scoring students. "If a selective college with an applicant pool of students with test scores in the top ten percent granted a preference to students with family incomes below $20,000, only one out of six would be black or Hispanic" (Kane, 1998:450). Kane concludes that there is an inescapable tradeoff between race blindness and racial diversity. Similar tradeoffs are evident throughout the system. For example, there are unavoidable tradeoffs be-

---

[1]At the University of California at Berkeley, for example, the number of minorities admitted for the 1998-1999 school year declined by almost 55 percent over the previous year's number (Wagner, 1998). Institutions affected by changed rules have worked hard to increase their minority enrollments through a variety of other means, the long-term effects of the changes and the institutions' responses are not yet clear.

tween the efficiency needed in reviewing large numbers of applications and the sensitivity to detail that the consideration of qualitative criteria requires. Composing any freshman class entails tradeoffs between the wishes of all constituencies: academic departments, development offices, alumni, athletic departments, etc. Indeed, every decision to select one student over others entails a tradeoff between the particular assets each individual might bring.

No ready solution to these dilemmas is apparent—there is currently no efficient tool for predicting the kinds of college success that are not directly measurable by grade point averages: campus leadership, persistence, intellectual curiosity, and the like. Without such a substitute, it is unclear what effects a wholesale deemphasizing of standardized admissions tests might have. The current admissions system is delicately balanced and, despite lawsuits and other signs of dissatisfaction, is arguably operating fairly well. The opportunity to attend a U.S. college is sought after by students from all over the world, and in an international context American higher education is viewed as a model of openness and accessibility.

If wholesale tradeoffs—between using tests heavily and not using them at all, for example—are not realistic, a focus on more particular ones could be useful. There are two kinds of errors that can occur in the college selection process: the selection of students who don't succeed and the failure to select students who would have succeeded. Because of the gap between majority and minority students' test scores, a greater proportion of minorities are rejected despite their capacity to succeed. It is possible to imagine modifications to the selection process that could result in reduction of this particular kind of error—rejection of able minority candidates—without undue disruption of the rate of correct decisions. In other words, any possible means of sorting high school students for college admissions will be imperfect—and yield error. It is institutions and their admissions staffs who make the errors—and have the responsibility to understand and minimize them.

Another way to think about the tradeoffs in the admissions process is to consider the range of specific targets that institutions might develop as they seek tools with which to meet broader institutional goals. Possible criteria include:

- support for institutional goals: a process that yields a student body able and willing to pursue academic and other goals defined by the institution;

- success for students and institutions: a process that yields high graduation rates, freshman grades, and life success (income) or fewer students who require remedial coursework, and attracts students likely to be admitted and succeed;

- fair representation: a process that yields a pool of candidates that is representative of the high school graduating class for the state or the nation;

- positive effects on secondary schools: a process that sends a clear signal about the kind of performance that is valued in college and aligns well with efforts to reform secondary education; and

- feasibility: a process that is easy to administer and manage, inexpensive to students and institutions, and accessible to students in all high schools.

In sum, the need to sort large numbers of students into a range of slots, the most desirable of which are limited, entails necessary tradeoffs between efficiency and accuracy, efficiency and responsiveness, and institutional mission and individual expectations.

Consideration of the multiple tradeoffs inherent in the task of sorting students for college leads the steering committee to conclude that the hope for a magic solution to current controversies and confusion is futile. These tradeoffs can be resolved only by human judgment, applied to particular circumstances. The committee hopes, however, that as institutions assess their goals and practices, they will move, individually and collectively, toward a system less fraught with mystery and injustice, both real and perceived. Clear understanding of the tradeoffs that go with both existing practices and any possible modifications to them will be the best guide to improving the admissions process for higher education in the United States.

Topics for Further Study

The charge to the steering committee was a narrow one within a complicated set of issues, and in the course of the workshop and the deliberations that led to this report a number of related topics that merit further attention emerged. This is by no means a comprehensive list of the topics that deserve further work, and the committee is well aware that these and other issues are already being explored in many contexts around the country. However, this report is intended in part as a spur to further discussion of unresolved issues surrounding admissions testing, and the committee notes a few of the questions about which further data and research would be particularly useful.

• Beyond the survey data cited in this report, what is known about the range of practices in admissions offices around the country? To what extent are test scores being used in inappropriate ways? Is it possible to obtain this information, given both institutions' reluctance to reveal the details of their practice, as well as practical constraints on the collection of detailed, comprehensive data?

• In the past decade, test preparation courses have proliferated and raised a number of issues. Some research has been done to determine the extent to which coaching can increase scores, but it is not definitive. An objective assessment of the effects of various coaching methods on scores is clearly needed. Are the numbers of coached students sufficient for there to have been a discernable effect on aggregate scores? If these courses have even a small effect on scores, they also raise important questions about test validity. How does the content of coaching programs relate to the subject domains the tests are designed to measure? Coaching also raises questions about fairness: such programs generally cost hundreds or thousands of dollars, and while some public school districts have offered coaching to their students, it is clearly not equally available to all.

• What is known about the relationship between varying uses of admissions test scores and K-12 education, particularly efforts to reform it? To what extent can uses of test scores be modified to offset the tendency of scores to reinforce the cumulative advantages and disadvantages that students are subject to in the K-12 years?

• Do the tests currently used measure constructs that are genuinely relevant to the academic programs for which they serve as screens? Has the content of the current tests been objectively evaluated in terms of current knowledge about human thinking and learning?

• To what extent are questions surrounding the use of admissions tests the same for graduate and professional school programs as they are for undergraduate institutions?

• What have been the effects of reliance on alternative means of selecting students? What alternative predictive tools have been used and what is known about them?

• What effects—on the composition of classes, on other aspects of the admissions process, on the tests themselves, for example—might be expected if a greater number of schools deemphasized or stopped requiring test scores?

• What measures could improve understanding of the benefits and limitations of admissions tests and reduce the risk of misuse of test scores? What steps could test makers, accreditation associations, higher education associations, and others take to ensure that sound test use policies are developed and followed?

References

American Educational Research Association, American Psychological Association, National Council on Measurement in Education, and National Council on Measurement in Education

    1985   *Standards for Educational and Psychological Testing*. Washington, DC: American Psychological Association.

    1998   *Draft Standards for Educational and Psychological Testing*. Washington, DC: American Psychological Association.

Bowen, W.G., and D. Bok

    1998   *The Shape of the River: Long-Term Consequences of Considering Race in College and University Admissions*. Princeton, NJ: Princeton University Press.

Breland, H.M.

    1998   National Trends in the Use of Test Scores in College Admissions. Available from Educational Testing Service, Princeton, NJ.

Breland, H.M., J. Maxey, G.T. McLure, M.J. Valigo, M.A. Boatwright, V.L. Ganley, and L.M. Jenkins

    1995   *Challenges in College Admissions: A Report of a Survey of Undergraduate Admission Policies, Practices, and Procedures*. American Association of Collegiate Registrars and Admissions Officers, American College Testing, The College Board, Educational Testing Service, and National Association of College Admission Counselors.

Jencks, C.

    1998   Racial bias in testing. In *The Black-White Test Score Gap*, C. Jencks and M. Phillips, editors. Washington, DC: Brookings Institution.

Johnson, S.T.

    1998   *True Scores, Consequences, and People: Tests and Their Impact on Selection and Educational Progress of Minorities*. Available from the Department of Human Development and Psychoeducational Studies, Howard University.

Kane, T.J.

    1998   Racial and ethnic preferences in college admissions. In *The Black-White Test Score Gap*, C. Jencks and M. Phillips, eds. Washington, DC: Brookings Institution.

Lemann, N.

    1995a The great sorting. *The Atlantic Monthly* 276(3)(September):84-100.

    1995b The structure of success in America. *The Atlantic Monthly* 276(2)(August): 41-60.

Lucas, S.R.

    1998   Prominent Explanations and Potential Prominent Factors in the Black/White Test Score Gap. Available from Sociology Department, University of California, Berkeley.

Messick, S.

    1993   Validity. In *Educational Measurement*, Third Edition, R. Linn, ed. Washington, DC: American Council on Education.

National Center for Education Statistics
  1997a *Access to Postsecondary Education for the 1992 High School Graduates.* L. Berkner. Washington, DC: U.S. Department of Education.
  1997b *Digest of Education Statistics.* Washington, DC: U.S. Department of Education.
  1998a College access and affordability. In *The Condition of Education.* Washington, DC: U.S. Department of Education.
  1998b Fall Enrollment in Postsecondary Institutions 1996. E.D. Tabs. NCES 1999- 239. Washington, DC: U.S. Department of Education.
National Research Council
  1982 *Ability Testing: Uses, Consequences, and Controversies. Part 1: Report of the Committee.* A. Wigdor and W.R. Garner, eds. Committee on Ability Testing, Commission on Behavioral and Social Sciences and Education, National Research Council. Washington, DC: National Academy Press.
  1999 *High Stakes: Testing for Tracking, Promotion, and Graduation.* J.P. Heubert and R.M. Hauser, eds. Committee on Appropriate Test Use, Board on Testing and Assessment, National Research Council. Washington, DC: National Academy Press.
Steele, C.M.
  1997 How stereotypes shape intellectual identity and performance. *American Psychological Association* 55(6):613-629.
Steele, C.M., and J. Aronson
  1995 Stereotype threat and the intellectual test performance of African Americans. *Journal of Personality and Social Psychology* 69(5):797-811.
U.S. Congress, Office of Technology and Assessment
  1992 *Testing in American Schools: Asking the Right Questions.* Office of Technology Assessment, OTA-SET-519. Washington, DC: U.S. Government Printing Office.
Vars, F.M., and W.G. Bowen
  1998 Scholastic aptitude test scores, race, and academic performance in selective colleges and universities. In *The Black-White Test Score Gap,* C. Jencks and M. Phillips, eds. Washington, DC: Brookings Institution.
Wagner, V.
  1998 Minority admissions plunge 55% at Cal. *San Francisco Examiner* April 1.
Wightman, L.F., and R.M. Jaeger
  1998 High Stakes and Ubiquitous Presence: An Overview and Comparison of *Standards for Educational and Psychological Testing.* Washington, DC: American Psychological Association. The ACT Assessment Program and the SAT Program. Available from University of North Carolina, Educational Research Methodology.
Willingham, W.W.
  1998 Validity in College Selection: Context and Evidence. Available from Educational Testing Service, Princeton, NJ.

Appendix A

Agenda

The Role of Tests in Higher Education Admissions

A National Research Council Workshop
sponsored by
the Board on Testing and Assessment and the
Office of Scientific and Engineering Personnel

DECEMBER 17 - Wyndham Bristol Hotel, 2430 Pennsylvania Avenue,
202-955-6400

8:30 am   **Welcome and Introduction**

This workshop is designed as a preliminary exploration of key issues in the debate over the rational role of standardized test results in the selection of students for college. Its purpose is to assist BOTA and OSEP in examining the proper role of test data in higher education admissions, and in identifying directions for further investigation.

     M.R.C. Greenwood, University of California,
         Santa Cruz, chair, OSEP
     Robert Linn, University of Colorado, Boulder,
         chair, BOTA

8:45 am   **Defining Successful Students and Institutional Goals**

Moderator: Robert Linn

Presentation: What is the range of successful college performance across institutions? How do schools determine which questions they want answered about applicants?

     Thomas Kane, Kennedy School, Harvard University

Discussion:
Richard Atkinson, University of California
Maryanne Fox, North Carolina State University

9:45 am   Break

10:00 am   Demystifying the Numbers
Moderator: John Wiley, University of Wisconsin,
Madison

Paper: High Stakes and Ubiquitous Presence: An
Overview and Comparison of the ACT Assessment
Program and the SAT program.
    Richard Jaeger, University of North Carolina
    Linda Wightman, University of North Carolina

Paper: National Trends in the Use of Test Scores in
College Admissions
    Hunter Breland, Educational Testing Service

Discussion: Are the uses of test results consistent with the
intentions of the examiners?
    Discussants: Nancy Cole, Educational Testing Service
                   Richard Ferguson, American College
                     Testing
                   Howard Everson, The College Board

12:00 pm   LUNCH

Current Practices and Their Impacts
Moderators:
Michael Kirst, Stanford University
William Taylor, Attorney at Law

**1:00 pm   *Paper:* Validity in College Selection: Context and
Evidence**
    Warren Willingham, Educational Testing Service

Paper: True Scores, Consequences, and People: Tests and
Their Impact on Selection and Educational Progress of
Minorities
    Sylvia Johnson, Howard University
    Discussant: Gary Natriello, Columbia University

2:00 pm   Break

2:15 pm   *Presentation:* Rethinking Selection in the Current Legal
Environment
Susan Sturm, University of Pennsylvania Law School
Discussion

3:30 pm   *Panel Discussion:* Admissions officers reflect on political,
practical, and legal pressures that affect the selection
process
David Cuttino, Tufts University
Thomas Parker, Williams College
Robert Seltzer, University of Wisconsin

4:30 pm   **Adjourn**

DECEMBER 18 – National Academy of Sciences, 2101 Constitution
Ave., 202-334-1578

Current Practices and Their Impacts (continued)

8:30 am   *Paper:* Prominent Explanations and Potential Prominent
Factors in the Black/White Test Score Gap
Samuel Lucas, University of California, Berkeley

Discussion: Is the predictive validity of test scores
sufficient to outweigh evidence of disparate impact?
Discussants: David Breneman, University of Virginia
Stacy Berg Dale, The Andrew Mellon
Foundation
Meredith Phillips, UCLA
Debra Stewart, North Carolina
State University

Moderator: Christopher Edley, Harvard Law School

10:15 am   **Break**

Alternatives and Supplements to Testing
Moderator: Carlos Gutierrez, California State
University, Los Angeles

10:30 am   *Presentation:* Current practices on University of
California campuses
    Dennis Galligani, University of California

Panel Discussion: Admissions officers reflect on
promising alternatives and supplements to test scores
    David Conley, University of Oregon
    William Hiss, Bates College
    Robert Seltzer, University of Wisconsin
    Audrey Smith, Hampshire College
    Peter Van Buskirk, Franklin and Marshall College

12:30 pm   **LUNCH**

1:30 pm   *Panel Discussion:* Perspectives on the practical and
policy issues associated with the selection process
    Moderator: Robert Linn

    Daniel Koretz, Boston College
    Ronald Latanision, Massachusetts Institute of
      Technology
    Susan Sturm, University of Pennsylvania
    Thomas Kane, Kennedy School, Harvard University

3:00 pm   *Synthesis and Reflections on Next Steps*

    Moderators: M.R.C. Greenwood and Robert Linn

3:30 pm   **Adjourn**

Appendix B

Participants

The Role of Tests in Higher Education Admissions
December 17-18, 1998

A National Research Council Workshop
sponsored by
the Board on Testing and Assessment and the
Office of Scientific and Engineering Personnel

Steering Committee

Christopher F. Edley, Jr., Harvard Law School, BOTA
M.R.C. Greenwood, University of California, Santa Cruz, OSEP
Carlos G. Gutierrez, California State University, L.A., OSEP
Michael W. Kirst, Stanford University, BOTA
Robert L. Linn, University of Colorado, BOTA
John D. Wiley, University of Wisconsin, Madison, OSEP

Presenters

Richard C. Atkinson,★ University of California
Hunter Breland, Educational Testing Service
David Breneman, University of Virginia
Nancy Cole, Educational Testing Service
David Conley, University of Oregon
David Cuttino, Tufts University
Stacey Berg Dale, The Andrew Mellon Foundation
Richard Ferguson, American College Testing
Maryanne Fox, North Carolina State University
Dennis Galligani, University of California

★ Member of BOTA

William Hiss, Bates College
Richard Jaeger,★ University of North Carolina
Sylvia Johnson, Howard University
Thomas Kane, JFK School of Government, Harvard University
Daniel Koretz, Boston College
Ron Latanision, Massachusetts Institute of Technology
Samuel Lucas, University of California, Berkeley
Gary Natriello, Columbia University - Teacher's College
Thomas Parker, Williams College
Meredith Phillips, University of California, Los Angeles
Robert Seltzer, University of Wisconsin, Madison
Audrey Smith, Hampshire College
Debra Stewart, North Carolina State University
Donald Stewart, The College Board
Susan Sturm, University of Pennsylvania
Peter Van Buskirk, Franklin and Marshall College
Linda Wightman, University of North Carolina, Greensboro
Warren Willingham, Educational Testing Service

Guests

Kimberly Adedovin, CRESPAR
Brenda Ashford, Association of American Medical Colleges
Kathie Bailey, Association of American Universities
Vicki Barr, Heath Resource Center
Lina Bell, George Washington University
Lois Bergeisen, Association of American Medical Colleges
David Berkowitz, U.S. Department of Education
Susan Bowers, U.S. Department of Education
Ellen Burbank, Pew Charitable Trusts
Janell Byrd, NAACP Legal Defense Fund
Donald Carstensen, ACT, Inc.
Duncan Chaplin, Urban Institute
Ella Cleveland, Association of American Medical Colleges
Arthur Coleman, U.S. Department of Education
Bridget Curran, National Governors' Association
Susan Duby, National Science Foundation
Lisa Evans, U.S. Department of Justice
John Folkins, Univerity of Iowa

Heather Roberts Fox, American Psychological Association
John Fry, U.S. Department of Education
Terry Fuller, Wakefield High School
Sandra Garcia, U.S. Department of Education
Dale Gough, AACRAO
John Hackett, Association of American Medical Colleges
Jane Hannaway, Urban Institute
Eileen Hanrahan, U.S. Department of Education
Patrick Hayashi, University of California
Kristen Huff, Association of American Medical Colleges
Gerunda Hughes, Howard University
Ellen Julian, Association of American Medical Colleges
Ernest Kimmel, Educational Testing Service
Judy Koenig Association of American Medical Colleges
Adina Kole, U.S. Department of Education
Rebecca Kopriva, U.S. Department of Education
Carole Lacampagne, U.S. Department of Education
Daniel Levin, Association of Governing Boards of Universities and
    Colleges
Cathy Lewis, U.S. Department of Education
Sharon Lewis, Council of Great City Schools
Jo-Anne Manswell, CRESPAR
Wayne Martin, Council of Chief State School Officers
Patricia McAllister, Educational Testing Service
Ron Millar, National Research Council
Daniel Minchew, ACT, Inc.
John Moore, U.S. Department of Justice
Jill Morrison, National Women's Law Center
Casey Mulqueen, American Institutes for Research
Jeryl Mumpower, National Science Foundation
Maureen Murphy, MathTech, Inc.
Karen Kovacs North, University of California, Santa Cruz
Beth O'Neil, Law School Admission Council
Leroy Outlaw, Lake Braddock Secondary Schools
Peter Pashley, Law School Admission Council
Peggy Peagler, CRESPAR
Nancy Petersen, ACT, Inc.
Robert Schaeffer, National Center for Fair and Open Testing
Cynthia Board Schmeiser, ACT, Inc.

Stephen Schreiber, Law School Admission Council
Theodore Shaw, NAACP Legal Defense Fund
Nevzer Stacey, U.S. Department of Education
David Sweet, U.S. Department of Education
William Taylor, Attorney at Law
Sheila Thompson, CRESPAR
Andrea Thornton, Law School Admission Council
William Trent, University of Illinois
Gabrielo Uro, Council of Great City Schools
Rebekah Tosado, U.S. Department of Education
Joan Van Tol, Law School Admission Council
Michael Wallace, CRESPAR
Kimberly West-Faulcon, NAACP Legal Defense Fund
Heshima White, U.S. Department of Justice
Deborah Wilds, American Council on Education
Adriane Williams, Council of Great City Schools
Lauress Wise,★ Human Resources Research Organization

NRC Staff

Marilyn Baker, Office of Science and Engineering Personnel
Stephen Baldwin, Board on Testing and Assessment
Alexandra Beatty, Board on Testing and Assessment
Meryl Bertenthal, Board on Testing and Assessment
Naomi Chudowsky, Board on Testing and Assessment
Joan Ferrini-Mundy, Center for Science, Mathematics and Engineering
    Education
Michael Feuer, Director, Board on Testing and Assessment
Cadelle Hemphill, Board on Testing and Assessment
Michele Kipke, Division on Social and Economic Studies
Lee Jones, Board on Testing and Assessment
Charlotte Kuh, Director, Office of Science and Engineering Personnel
Karen Mitchell, Board on Testing and Assessment
Patricia Morison, Board on Testing and Assessment